CONTENTS

KU-786-435

Words that appear in the text in bold, **like this**, are explained in the Glossary.

WHAT IS A CONTINENT?

The Earth has seven very large areas of land called **continents**. Some are surrounded by oceans, such as Antarctica. Other continents are joined together, such as North and South America. Continents usually have many countries and different peoples living in them.

Most continents have different **environments**, with many types of plants and animals living in them. When you look at an entire continent at once, you can see how weather, living things, and the land all fit together.

Did you know?
The exact centre of North America is Rugby, North Dakota. The people who live there have put a large stone marker on the spot.

This map shows the seven continents of the world.

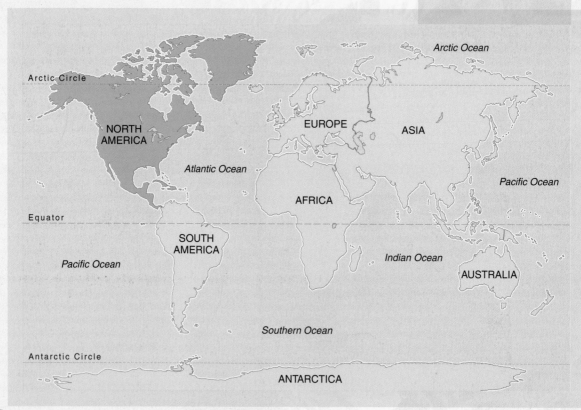

9010845834

EXPLORING CONTINENTS

NORTH AMERICA

Tristan Boyer Binns

Heinemann
LIBRARY

www.heinemann.co.uk/library
Visit our website to find out more information about Heinemann Library books.

To order:
 Phone 44 (0) 1865 888066
 Send a fax to 44 (0) 1865 314091
 Visit the Heinemann Bookshop at www.heinemann.co.uk/library to browse our catalogue and order online.

First published in Great Britain by Heinemann, Halley Court, Jordan Hill, Oxford, OX2 8EJ, part of Harcourt Education.

© Harcourt Education Ltd 2007
First published in paperback in 2008
The moral right of the proprietor has been asserted.

All rights reserved. No part of this publication may be reproduced, stored in a retrieval system, or transmitted in any form or by any means, electronic, mechanical, photocopying, recording, or otherwise, without either the prior written permission of the publishers or a licence permitting restricted copying in the United Kingdom issued by the Copyright Licensing Agency Ltd, 90 Tottenham Court Road, London W1T 4LP (www.cla.co.uk).

Editorial: Louise Galpine and Harriet Milles
Design: Richard Parker and Q2A Solutions
Illustrations: Jeff Edwards
Picture Research: Mica Brancic and Beatrice Ray
Production: Camilla Crask

Originated by Chroma
Printed and bound in China by WKT

13 digit ISBN 978 0431 09747 3 (hardback)
11 10 09 08 07
10 9 8 7 6 5 4 3 2 1

13 digit ISBN 978 0 431 09755 8 (paperback)
12 11 10 09 08
10 9 8 7 6 5 4 3 2 1

British Library Cataloguing in Publication Data
Binns, Tristan Boyer
North America. - (Exploring continents)
1.North America - Geography - Juvenile literature
917
A full catalogue record for this book is available from the British Library.

Acknowledgements
Alamy p. 23 (Bryan and Cherry Alexander); Corbis pp. 17 (James L. Amos), 27; Getty pp. 8 (Imagebank), 9 (Art Wolfe), 10 (Imagebank), 13 (Iconica), 14 (National Geographic), 15 (National Geographic), 18 (Taxi), 19 (Photographer's Choice/Sylvain Grandadam), 24 (Hulton); Lonely Planet Images pp. 7 (Greg Gawlowski), 11 (Lee Foster), 22, 25 (Richard I'Anson); Science Photo Library p. 5 (Planetary Visions Ltd); Travel Ink p. 21.

Cover satellite image of North America reproduced with permission of SPL/M-Sat Ltd.

Every effort has been made to contact copyright holders of any material reproduced in this book. Any omissions will be rectified in subsequent printings if notice is given to the publishers.

East Riding of Yorkshire Library and Information Services

901 084583 4	
Askews	
917	£6.99
MAR	

North America

North America is the third largest continent in the world, with the fourth largest population. It contains three very large countries – Canada, the United States, and Mexico – and twenty smaller countries. Of these, seven countries are found on a narrow strip of land called Central America. The rest are on islands in the Caribbean Sea.

The Atlantic and Pacific Oceans run down the sides of the North American continent. The Gulf of Mexico is to the south and the Arctic Ocean is to the north.

You can find many **contrasts** in North America. There are great mountain peaks and sandy coasts. There are also cities packed with people and thousands of miles of countryside where no one lives. Some of the people are rich and others are very poor.

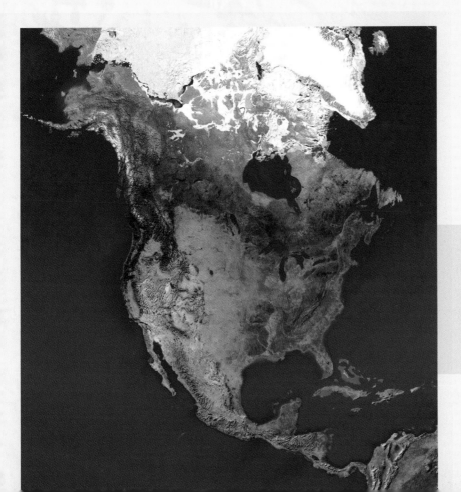

Look at North America from space. You can see the mountain ranges, the icy north and the hot rainforests in the south.

WHAT DOES NORTH AMERICA LOOK LIKE?

To the north

At the very north of the continent there is an ice sheet. It covers Greenland and keeps many of the islands in northern Canada icy cold.

To the east

North America has mountains running from the north to the south on both sides of the continent. The best-known of the ranges on the eastern side is the Appalachians.

Below the Appalachians to the east is a flat, wide section called the Coastal Plain. It has swamps and marshes at its ocean edges and forests further inland.

This map shows some of the dramatic natural features found in North America.

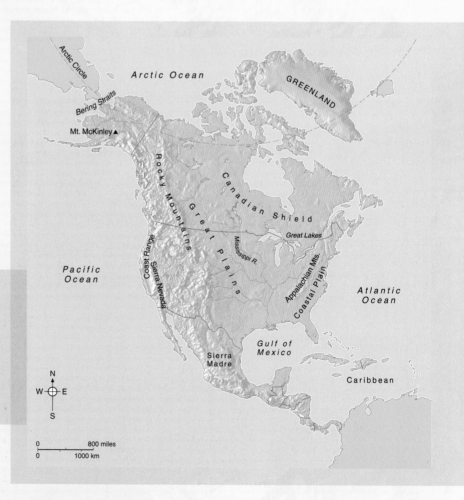

To the west

On the west side of the continent you will find the Rocky Mountains, the Sierra Nevadas, and the Sierra Madres. A special feature of these mountains is the Continental Divide. People sometimes call it the backbone of North America. All the rivers to the west of the Continental Divide flow to the Pacific Ocean. All the rivers to the east flow to the Atlantic Ocean.

The Rocky Mountains have vast stretches of wilderness where plants and animals live.

Did you know?

Volcanoes made some of the mountains in North America. On May 18, 1980 a volcanic mountain in the Western Highlands erupted. It is called Mt. Saint Helens, and it created a huge disaster site. Enough trees were knocked down during the blast to have built 300,000 homes! A cloud of ash thrown out during the eruption circled the whole Earth in 15 days.

Flat lands

In between the two great mountain ranges in the north lies the Canadian Shield. This is a **plateau**, or a high flat piece of land. It has a lot of rock and forest, and is not used for farming.

South of the Canadian Shield is the area known as the Great Plains. This region is famous for having flat, fertile land. The wild landscape is called a **prairie**. Grass and wildflowers wave in the breezes. Where the prairie is cleared, farmers grow millions of **bushels** of wheat.

Some people call the Great Plains the breadbasket of the world.

NORTH AMERICA FACTS

- *Highest point:* Mt. McKinley (Denali) in Alaska: 6,194 m (20,320 ft)
- *Lowest point:* Death Valley National Park in California: 86 m (282 ft) below sea level
- *Biggest desert:* Chihuahuan Desert: 362,600 square km (140,000 square miles)
- *World's largest island:* Greenland: 2,175,600 square km (840,000 square miles)
- *World's largest freshwater lake:* Lake Superior (United States and Canada): 82,100 square km (31,700 square miles); water volume 12,100 cubic km (2,900 cubic miles)

Deserts and rainforests

In the west, **deserts** stretch from the US states of California, Nevada, and Utah down into Mexico. Rainforests begin in southern Mexico and are found throughout Central America. Many rainforests have been cut down for their wood and to make flat land for people to use. This has changed the environment for plants and animals a great deal.

Island life

In the Caribbean Sea there are thousands of islands that are part of North America. Cuba is the largest, but many of the islands are very small. The Bahamas alone has between 2,000 and 3,000 islands. Volcanoes formed some islands; others are made of coral and stone.

An incredible range of plants and animals live in the rainforests of Central America. From inside the soil to high up above the tops of the trees, life bursts out in the rainforest environment.

WHAT IS THE WEATHER LIKE IN NORTH AMERICA?

From the north to the south of North America there are extremes of **climate**. In parts of northern Canada and Greenland, the temperature never rises above freezing. In some places in Mexico and Central America, it never freezes.

Most of North America is **temperate**, which means it has moderate weather and four seasons. In the middle of the continent it is normal to have cold winters, wet springs, hot summers, and cool autumns. To the north, the climate is **arctic**, where it is cold even in summer. To the south, the climate is **tropical**. There, it is always warm and wet.

In the northeast of the USA, the leaves turn bright colours then fall off as autumn grows colder. The leaves grow back green when the days get longer and warmer in the spring.

The tropical climate brings tourists to the Caribbean islands. There, sugar cane and coffee grow easily. From summer through autumn this climate also brings hurricanes and big tropical storms.

Highs and lows

As you go higher up, the climate changes, too. Mountains and high plateaus are colder and have fewer trees. In North America, the highest mountains are often warm and covered with forests at the base, but the peaks can have snow on them all year round.

NORTH AMERICA FACTS

- *Hottest recorded temperature:* Death Valley National Park, California: 57°C (134°F)
- *Coldest recorded temperature:* Northice, Greenland: minus 66°C (minus 87°F)
- *Highest average rainfall:* Henderson Lake, British Columbia: 656 cm (256 inches) in a year
- *Lowest average rainfall:* Batagues, Mexico: 3.1 cm (1.2 inches) in a year
- *Most rainfall in the world in less than an hour:* Holt, Montana: 30.5 cm (12 inches) in 42 minutes

WHAT PLANTS AND ANIMALS LIVE IN NORTH AMERICA?

North America has such a range of climates that an amazing number of different kinds of plants live across the continent. Each lives in a **habitat** that suits its needs. Far north, only a few kinds of plants can stand the cold and ice. They are mostly small, such as moss and lichens. In the tropical south, thousands of kinds of plants thrive. Trees in the rainforest can grow over 50 metres (165 feet) tall! A great deal of North America is covered with forests. There are coniferous, evergreen fir trees and deciduous trees that lose their leaves each winter.

Plants and animals

All animals depend on plants for food. Where there are many kinds of plants, there are also many kinds of animals and insects. Over the years, they have learned how to help each other out. Bees all over North America **pollinate** flowers. In the desert, bats drink the nectar made by giant cacti flowers. They spread the flowers' pollen which helps the cacti to make seeds.

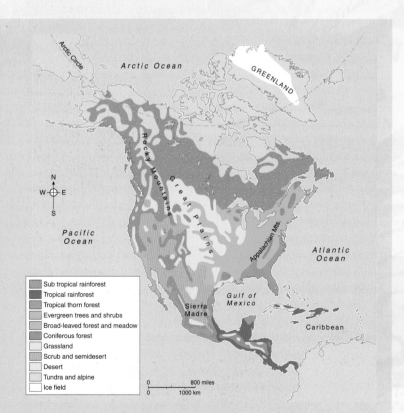

Sub tropical rainforest
Tropical rainforest
Tropical thorn forest
Evergreen trees and shrubs
Broad-leaved forest and meadow
Coniferous forest
Grassland
Scrub and semidesert
Desert
Tundra and alpine
Ice field

Many types of plants and animals live in the different climates of North America.

The rainforest environment

There are more types of trees, birds, insects, and fish in a patch of tropical rainforest than in any other kind of environment. About four-fifths of what we eat originally came from the rainforests – even potatoes and chocolate. Many of the drugs we use to treat diseases come from rainforest plants. We also rely on rainforest trees to clean the air for the whole planet. When the rainforests are cleared, these plants and animals are often lost forever.

In the northwest, grizzly bears roam the forests. The bears catch salmon as they swim upstream to lay their eggs in late summer.

Did you know?

The jaguar is the biggest cat in North America. It grows up to 2.6 m (nearly 9 feet) long and can weigh as much as 158 kg (348 lbs). It lives in thick tropical forests in Mexico and Central America.

Desert plants

Plants such as cactus and the Mexican jumping bean shrub grow in the dry rocky deserts of the American southwest and Mexican north. The jumping bean makes a seed pod that the jumping bean moth loves. The baby moths are tiny worm-like **larvae** that live in the pod and eat the seed. Then they throw themselves around inside the pod, making it jump! In the end, the larvae spin **cocoons** inside the pod, turn into moths, and eat their way out. Some people make a living collecting the jumping beans and selling them.

Cactus plants are excellent water hoarders. When it rains, the cactus stores extra water. The ribs along its trunk swell out as it fills with water. It looks almost smooth when it is full.

The bison

The bison is also known as the buffalo. It is a **native** to the North American plains. Many Native Americans hunted bison. They used their meat, **hides**, and even **dung** for everything from food and clothing to fuel and shelter. About 200 years ago, there were millions of bison thundering over the plains. Settlers killed them because they made trouble for farming and railways. Now there are very few left.

Bald eagles can be found all over the northern forests. The eagles need tall trees to build their huge nests. When their habitat is threatened, they can't raise their chicks.

The pronghorn

The pronghorn is a bit like a deer or an antelope. It is unique to North America. It is the fastest animal in the western hemisphere. It can run at 60 mph (97 kph) and keep going almost that quickly for hours. It lives in grassland and deserts and can survive temperatures of 54°C to minus 46°C (130°F to minus 50°F).

WHAT ARE NORTH AMERICA'S NATURAL RESOURCES?

There are many **natural resources** in North America. There are **minerals** mined out of the ground, plants grown as crops, and animals reared or caught for food. North America has enough natural resources to support the millions of people who live there, although some goods are still imported.

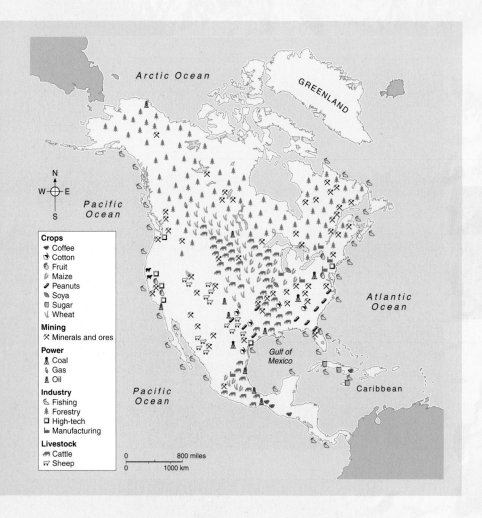

Crops
- ☕ Coffee
- 🌿 Cotton
- 🍎 Fruit
- 🌽 Maize
- 🥜 Peanuts
- 🫘 Soya
- ▣ Sugar
- 🌾 Wheat

Mining
- ⚒ Minerals and ores

Power
- 🏭 Coal
- 🛢 Gas
- 🛢 Oil

Industry
- 🎣 Fishing
- 🌲 Forestry
- 💻 High-tech
- 🏭 Manufacturing

Livestock
- 🐄 Cattle
- 🐑 Sheep

0 — 800 miles
0 — 1000 km

This map shows some of the natural resources and industries in North America.

Cotton crops

Cotton is grown in the warm southern states of the USA and in Mexico. Raw cotton is sold to be made into thread (yarn) and cloth. The yarn and cloth are then used to make clothing.

Iron into cars

Iron is a raw material that is mined from the ground. Where iron is found in the United States, you will also find **industries** that turn iron into steel. Steel is a material used to make machines, such as cars. Detroit, in the US state of Michigan, grew into a big car-making area because of the raw materials near by. By 1900 it had some of the best transport links to the rest of the United States. Cars made there were easily shipped elsewhere to be sold.

The waterways and railways make it easy to move materials and goods around in Detroit. With all the industry came many people and a great deal of pollution, too.

Did you know?

North America needs a lot of energy to run its many industries and support people's lives. It makes a great deal of the world's energy, too. In 1999, North America accounted for around:

- 19 per cent of world oil production
- 31 per cent of world natural gas production
- 25 per cent of world coal production
- 32 per cent of world electricity generation.

Making food

Farmers grow food throughout North America. Warmer climates are good for growing fruit and vegetables, which are sold in shops. Some of the crops, such as wheat, need to be **processed** before they are eaten. Wheat is ground and then baked into bread. **Maize** is grown to feed people and animals. Beef cattle fed on maize are butchered and their meat is sold for food in shops and restaurants. Many people earn a living while making and processing raw materials into finished goods.

Making ideas

Some people use their skills to make machines that do work for us. In North America, the computer software industry makes programmes and games that are used all over the world.

Forestry is an important industry in Canada. Growing and harvesting trees must be done carefully so the forests stay healthy. The wood is used to build houses and furniture.

Did you know?

The gross national product is the total value of everything made in a country. The USA has the highest in the world. Its gross national product is seven times that of all the other countries in North America put together.

WHAT CITIES AND COUNTRIES ARE IN NORTH AMERICA?

Canada

North America is broken up into 23 countries. Canada is the biggest and the furthest north. It is the second largest country in the world. The far north of Canada is cold and hard to live in. It is still **frontier** land. Most Canadians live in the south of the country, near the border with the United States.

The United States

The United States is the second largest country in North America, but it has the most people. Its cities are very crowded. Most people live on the two coasts. In between there are some cities and also wide-open spaces of wilderness. There are almost nine times more people in the USA than in Canada.

Mexico

Mexico is south of the United States. It is a long thin country with mountains and deserts.

In the 1700s, Toronto was just a small trading post on the north shore of Lake Ontario. Now it is Canada's largest city.

This map shows the countries and major cities of North America.

Smaller countries

The smaller countries and territories in North America have fewer **ecosystems**. They often have fewer kinds of industry, too. The islands in the Caribbean Sea and the coasts of Mexico and Central America have beautiful beaches. They rely on tourism for money, and many holiday resorts have been built there. Being exposed to the sea also means that powerful storms and hurricanes can hit hard.

In North America most of the people who live in the more southern countries are farmers. They have less money than many of the people in the more northern countries. One of the reasons for this is that making raw materials tends to earn less money than selling finished goods. This means that growing food makes less money than selling meals in a restaurant.

Other governments

South of Mexico are seven countries that make up Central America. Most of these are **democracies**, where the people elect the country's rulers.

The countries of Canada, Belize, and Jamaica amongst others are also part of the **British Commonwealth**. This means that they rule themselves, but the United Kingdom's king or queen is their **head of state**.

There are fourteen island countries in North America. Some of the Caribbean islands are democracies, such as Haiti and the Dominican Republic. Many are **overseas territories** of other, larger countries which govern them. The Cayman Islands in the Caribbean is a British overseas territory.

There are also islands near Canada that are French territories. Greenland in the icy far north governs itself, but is still part of the Kingdom of Denmark.

Havana in Cuba is famous for its music, food, and nightlife.

Biggest cities

There are many big cities in North America. Most have grown up over time where transport and industry were strong. The largest include Mexico City in Mexico, New York City, Los Angeles, Chicago, and Houston in the United States, and Toronto and Montréal in Canada. Almost 9 million people live in Mexico City. Only about 40,000 people live in the whole of one of the Caribbean island countries, St Kitts.

Working together

The countries in a continent sometimes need to work together to agree on things that affect them all. They decide how to trade with each other. They agree how best to use the waters off their coasts.

Mexico City is the largest city in North America, but only the twelfth largest city in the world.

Did you know?

The state of Hawaii is not part of the continent of North America, even though it is part of the USA!

WHO LIVES IN NORTH AMERICA?

There are hundreds of different groups of peoples living in North America. Each country also has its own **culture** and **traditions**.

Native Americans

The first people to live in North America probably walked there across a land bridge over the Bering Straits where the US state of Alaska meets Asia. This was over 15,000 years ago. Then the **ice age** ended and the sea level rose as the ice melted. Slowly the land bridge was covered by water. The people moved out over the continent. They **adapted** to their new environments, learning the best ways to live there. They spoke hundreds of different languages. These people are now called Native Americans.

The native peoples of the Arctic have learned how best to survive in the cold. The Inuit peoples have lived in the Arctic for thousands of years. They still keep some of their old ways of life, such as using dogs to pull their sledges.

European settlers

About 500 years ago, people from Europe started settling in North America. At first there was a rush to set up **colonies** and claim **territory**. The British, French, Spanish, and Dutch all took or bought land from the native peoples. Over time they founded new countries:

- People from Britain and France settled in Canada.

- British, Spanish, French, and Dutch colonies eventually became the United States.

- The Spanish settled in Mexico and Central America.

The European settlers brought their religions and languages with them. Most of the people in North America are now Christian, either Protestant or Catholic. The main languages are English, Spanish, and French.

The Dutch first settled Manhattan Island in 1624. Later, they bought the island from the Native Americans for very little money. This area later became New York City.

Did you know?

In the United States, Canada, and Mexico, there are about:
- 176 million Catholic Christians
- 169 million Protestant Christians
- 4.5 million Jews
- 1.7 million Muslims

Struggles between natives and settlers

There were many struggles and wars between the natives and European settlers. Many Native Americans were forced to move, or were killed by war or disease. But in some places, native peoples still live in their traditional homelands. Native Americans make up almost half the population of Guatemala today. Many native peoples in North America married and had children with European settlers. Today, millions of people have a mixed patchwork of **ancestors**!

New immigrants

For hundreds of years, North American countries have welcomed new **immigrants**. These people have added their languages, religions, and ways of life to the continent. In the United States, German and Scandinavian farmers came to the Northeast and Midwest, and Chinese and Japanese people came to the West Coast.

People also move between the countries in North America. Many Mexicans **emigrate** to the United States, and many Americans emigrate to Canada. Today, about 500 million people live in North America.

In Central American towns, market day is very important. Farmers and craftspeople bring their food and goods for people to buy. They can also catch up on the news in the surrounding villages.

WHAT FAMOUS PLACES ARE IN NORTH AMERICA?

North America is packed full of famous landmarks. Some are natural, such as Niagara Falls, Yellowstone's **geysers**, and the Chihuahuan Desert. The Grand Canyon in Arizona in the United States is a stunning sight. Millions of people visit it each year. These landmarks formed over millions of years as water, volcanoes, and wind shaped the land.

Old and modern attractions

Long ago, Native Americans made amazing buildings and statues in North America. Today, people can still visit the Mayan Pyramids in Mexico and Central America, or see how people lived hundreds of years ago in the cliff palaces at Mesa Verde in Colorado.

There are also some wonderful modern man-made structures to visit, such as the statues at Mount Rushmore in the US state of South Dakota. In Mexico City, there is a tall column with a golden angel on top called Winged Victory, or *El Angel*.

The statues at Mount Rushmore are truly huge! They show four U.S. presidents: George Washington, Thomas Jefferson, Theodore Roosevelt, and Abraham Lincoln.

Towers and bridges

There are some breathtaking towers and bridges in North America. The views from the top of the CN Tower in Toronto, Canada, and the Sears Tower in Chicago are fantastic. Many of the longest bridges in the world are in North America. One of these is the Lake Pontchartrain Causeway in the US state of Louisiana, which measures 38.4 km (23.8 miles).

The Panama Canal

The Panama Canal divides North America from South America. It lets boats travel from the Atlantic Ocean to the Pacific Ocean without having to go all the way around the southern tip of South America. It saves 14,484 kilometres (9,000 miles) on the trip from New York to San Francisco.

Did you know?

The Spanish first proposed building a Panama Canal about 500 years ago, but it wasn't completed until 1914! About 800,000 ships have travelled through it since then.

1 Bering Straits
2 Mt. St. Helens
3 Yellowstone
4 Yosemite
5 Hollywood
6 Mojave Desert
7 Grand Canyon
8 Mesa Verde
9 Chihuhuan Desert
10 Mt. Rushmore
11 Winged Victory Statue
12 Mayan Pyramids
13 Tikal
14 Panama Canal
15 Sears Tower
16 Lake Pontchartrain
17 Eire Canal, Niagara Falls and CN Tower
18 Statue of Liberty
19 Everglades

This map shows some of the amazing wonders found in North America.

27

CONTINENTS COMPARISON CHART

Continent	Area	Population	
AFRICA	30,365,000 square kilometres (11,720,000 square miles)	906 million	
ANTARCTICA	14,200,000 square kilometres (5,500,000 square miles)	officially none, but about 4,000 people live on the research stations during the summer and over 3,000 people visit as tourists each year. People have lived there for as long as three and a half years at a time.	
ASIA	44,614,000 square kilometres (17,226,200 square miles)	almost 4,000 million	
AUSTRALIA	7,713,364 square kilometres (2,966,136 square miles)	approximately 20,090,400 (2005 estimate)	
EUROPE	10,400,000 square kilometres (4,000,000 square miles)	approximately 727 million (2005 estimate)	
NORTH AMERICA	24,230,000 square kilometres (9,355,000 square miles)	approximately 509,915,000 (2005 estimate)	
SOUTH AMERICA	17,814,000 square kilometres (6,878,000 square miles)	380 million	

Number of Countries	Highest Point	Longest River
54 (includes Western Sahara)	Mount Kilimanjaro, Tanzania — 5,895 metres (19,340 feet)	Nile River — 6,695 kilometres (4,160 miles)
none, but over 23 countries have research stations in Antarctica	Vinson Massif — 4,897 metres (16,067 feet)	River Onyx — 12 kilometres (7.5 miles) **Biggest Ice Shelf** Ross Ice Shelf in western Antarctica — 965 kilometres (600 miles) long.
50	Mount Everest, Tibet and Nepal — 8,850 metres (29,035 feet)	Yangtze River, China — 6,300 kilometres (3,914 miles)
1	Mount Kosciusko — 2,229 metres (7,313 feet)	Murray River — 2,520 kilometres (1,566 miles)
47	Mount Elbrus, Russia — 5,642 metres (18,510 feet)	River Volga — 3,685 kilometres (2,290 miles)
23	Mount McKinley (Denali) in Alaska — 6,194 metres (20,320 feet)	Mississippi/Missouri River System — 6,270 kilometres (3,895 miles)
12	Aconcagua, Argentina — 6,959 metres (22,834 feet)	Amazon River — 6,400 kilometres (4,000 miles)

GLOSSARY

adapted learned to adjust to live the best way possible in a certain environment

ancestor someone you are linked to by birth, such as your parents or grandparents

arctic climate that is bitterly cold and gets little sun

British Commonwealth group of independent countries that govern themselves, but have the British king or queen as their head of state

bushel measurement of grain, about 8 gallons or 36 litres

climate how hot or cold, wet or dry, and windy or still a place is

cocoon covering or case of silk spun by a larvae to protect itself

colony settlement given money, supplies and military support by a home country usually far away

continent largest landmass on the globe

contrast difference between things that are very unlike each other, such as desert and swamp

culture features of a group of people that show how they live and what is most important to them

democracy government where people vote for and elect their leaders

desert place where very little rain falls year round

dung faeces or droppings

ecosystem all the plants and animals and the particular environment they live in

emigrate to leave your home country and move to a new country

environment place where a plant or animal lives, and how wet or dry, hot or cold it is

frontier place where there are very few people and most of the land is wilderness

geyser spring that shoots up jets of hot water

habitat place and conditions a living thing needs to survive

head of state person who is ruler of a country or group of countries

hide skin and fur of an animal

ice age time when ice covered most of the Earth's surface

immigrant person who chooses to move to and settle in a new country

industry business, usually making products for sale

larvae very young animal after it hatches from its egg and before it grows into an adult

maize grain food crop also known as corn

mineral non-living thing that can be mined from the Earth or sea and is used to make other things

native people, plants, or animals that are the first to live in a place

natural resources materials found in the Earth and sea that are used to make other things or for food

overseas territory place far from the country that rules it

plateau flat area of land, sometimes high up

pollinate fertilize a flower to make seeds

prairie fairly dry grassland with few trees

processed when raw materials are changed so they can be made into finished goods

temperate mild climate, not too cold or hot, or too wet or dry

territory defined area of land

tradition something that has been done for many years in a special way

tropical hot and wet climate

Books

America's Wetlands: Guide To Plants And Animals (America's Ecosystems), Marianne D. Wallace (Fulcrum Publishing, 2001)

Animals in Order series (Franklin Watts, 2003)

Biomes of North America series (Carolrhoda Books, 2004)

Exploration of North America, Shirley Greenway (Barron's Educational Series, 1998)

North America (Continents), Malcolm Porter and Keith Lye (Raintree, 2001)

North America (True Books: Continents), David Petersen (Children's Press, 1999)

On the Wing: American Birds in Migration, Carol Lerner (HarperCollins, 2001)

The Prairie (Ecosystems of North America), Alison Ormsby (Benchmark, 1998)

Trees of North America (Usborne Spotter's Guides), Alan Mitchell (Usborne, 1993)

Useful websites

- This is an interesting place to learn about North American plants:
  http://www.nanps.org/about/frame.shtml
- Here is the Smithsonian National Zoo site about North American animals:
  http://nationalzoo.si.edu/Animals/NorthAmerica/ForKids/default.cfm
- A game to test your knowledge about North American countries:
  http://www.playkidsgames.com/games/north%20americaCountries/default.htm#
- Another game, a jigsaw puzzle of North America:
  http://www.playkidsgames.com/games/north%20americaJigsaw/default.htm#
- This is all about early settlement in Canada:
  http://www.collectionscanada.ca/settlement/kids/021013-1500-e.html
- Greenpeace has a special Kids for Forests site, where you can learn how to help save ancient forests:
  http://archive.greenpeace.org/kidsforforests/about.html

Disclaimer

All the internet addresses (URLs) given in this book were valid at the time of going to press. However, due to the dynamic nature of the internet, some addresses may have changed, or sites may have ceased to exist since publication. While the author and publishers regret any inconvenience this may cause readers, no responsibility for such changes can be accepted by either the author(s) or the publishers.

INDEX